cupcakes

This edition published in 2011 by
CHARTWELL BOOKS, INC.
a division of BOOK SALES, INC.
276 Fifth Avenue Suite 206
New York, New York 10001
USA

This edition published by arrangement with Flame Tree Publishing,
an imprint of The Foundry Creative Media Company Limited
Crabtree Hall, Crabtree Lane
Fulham, London SW6 6TY
United Kingdom
www.flametreepublishing.com

Publisher's Note:
Raw or semi-cooked eggs should not be consumed by babies, toddlers, pregnant or breastfeeding
women, the elderly or those suffering from a chronic illness.

Publisher & Creative Director: Nick Wells
Senior Project Editor: Catherine Taylor
Photography: Colin Bowling
Home economist and stylist: Ann Nicol
Copy Editor: Constance Novis
Art Director: Mike Spender
Layout Design: Jane Ashley
Digital Design & Production: Chris Herbert

Special thanks to Digby Smith and Helen Wall, and to Squires Group and Lakeland for
supplying materials for photography.

ISBN: 978-0-7858-2737-5

Printed in China

cupcakes

Ann Nicol

CHARTWELL
BOOKS, INC.

Contents

Introduction

Why are cupcakes so popular? They seem to be on sale everywhere these days, but because these little cakes are so quick and easy (you will find that most of the recipes in this book take less than half an hour to bake), it is so simple to make your own. Cupcakes are delightful and versatile—ideal for an informal gathering, a special occasion, or for children's parties.

There is no comparison to the quality of homemade cakes and the fun you can have making and baking them, and, as shop-bought cakes are expensive, you will notice the difference in price too. You also have plenty of scope for decorating, so you can customize your treats for any occasion.

As a gift or a centerpiece, a batch of cupcakes brings a personal touch to any celebration, from a wedding anniversary to a children's party. This book has cakes for every occasion, some very quick and easy, some requiring a little more patience. If you are short of time, I have included tips on preparing ahead and freezing to make life easy.

Baking is a good way to introduce children to the art of cooking and these recipes will help you teach them the basic techniques. Children also love the decorating part, and there are lots of ideas here to choose from.

So, what is the best part of baking cupcakes? Well, they give so much pleasure—you get a real sense of satisfaction when you create a fresh batch of delicious cakes, accompanied by the marvelous aroma that fills your home. And just watch the delighted reaction when you give them to your friends and neighbors.

How to Use This Book

This book is aimed at both those new to baking and experienced bakers, and shows how to create these popular treats, from the right equipment and ingredients to the decoration.

Just follow our simple step-by-step guides to ensure successful results. The choice is yours—you can make large, standard or even mini cupcakes. The size of each cake will depend on the depth of the depressions in your pans and how deeply you fill the paper baking cups.

This book is divided into sections that deal with different types of cakes, including family favorites and cupcakes to have with a mid-morning coffee, luscious chocolate cupcakes, and cupcakes decorated for special occasions such as birthdays, Mother's Day, weddings, and Christmas. Baking and cake decoration involve many different techniques, and a little skill is needed for certain recipes, but you will build up your confidence through practice. To help you achieve success every time, there are tips on choosing the right type of muffin pan and paper baking cups. Using the very best ingredients is important, as are using proper utensils and careful weighing and

measuring. You will not achieve good results without first checking your oven for correct temperatures and exact timings (*see* below).

Check Your Oven

Each recipe begins with an oven setting, and it is important to preheat the oven to the correct temperature before placing the cupcakes in to bake. As well as preheating the oven, it is important to arrange the shelves in the correct position in the oven before you start. The best baking position for cupcakes is just above the center of the oven and best results are achieved by baking only one pan at a time. If you bake two pans at once, you may find the cakes in the pan on the lower shelf will come out with flatter tops.

Many of us have fan-assisted ovens. These circulate hot air around the oven and heat up very quickly. For fan ovens, you will need to reduce the temperature stated in the recipe by 25°F. For example, if the stated temperature in a recipe is 350°F, reduce it to 325°F for a fan-assisted oven. However, ovens do vary, so follow your manufacturer's instructions and get to know the way your oven heats. If your oven is too hot, the outsides will burn before the interior has had time to cook. If it is too cool, the cakes may sink or not rise evenly. Try not to open the oven door until at least halfway through the baking time, when the cupcakes will have had time to rise and set, because a sudden drop in temperature will stop the cakes from rising and they may sink.

Measuring

All spoon measurements should be used level for accuracy, and always use a set of measuring spoons specifically designed for measuring ingredients for cooking. Do not use domestic teaspoons and tablespoons because these may be deeper or shallower than a proper measuring spoon.

All cup measurements for dry ingredients must be level, unless the recipe specifies heaping or scant. Spoon dry ingredients into the appropriate measuring cup and level off any extra using the straight side of a metal spatula or knife.

A measuring cup is vital for liquids and it needs to be marked with small measures for smaller amounts.

Equipment and Utensils

Bakeware

Metal Muffin Pans

Muffin pans come in different sizes. The standard-size pan that we use here has 12 holes, about 1¼–1½ inches deep. Then there are pans with 'mini'-size holes (*see* right). If a recipe says, for example, 'Makes 10–12', you will make the smaller number if your cups are on the deeper end of 1¼–1½ inches.

Mini-muffin Pans

These have small individual holes (24 usually, or 12) that can be half the diameter of holes in the standard muffin pans, and as shallow as ¾ inch deep. They can be made of metal, but the silicone pans are particularly useful for mini muffins because they turn out so easily and give a good shape.

Silicone Muffin Pans and Silicone Baking Cups

These are flexible and produce very good results. Although they are sold as nonstick, it is still advisable to rub around the inside of each hole or cup with a little oil on some paper towel to prevent sticking. Individual silicone baking cups

When purchasing, buy the heaviest pan you can afford—although these will be expensive, they produce the best results because they distribute the heat well and do not buckle. If using pans without a nonstick finish, it is advisable to give these a light greasing before use. To grease pans, apply a thin film of melted vegetable margarine to each hole with a pastry brush or coat the inside of each hole by rubbing them with a little softened butter or margarine using some paper towels. You will normally need to line metal muffin pans with deep paper baking cups or strips of parchment paper.

come in many bright colors and, unlike paper baking cups, are reusable. Simply wash out any crumbs after use in soapy water and leave them to dry, or clean them in the dishwasher.

Paper Baking Cups

These come in many varieties, colors, and shapes. It is advisable to buy the more expensive types, which are thicker and give a good shape to the cupcake as it rises. Oil and moisture are less likely to penetrate the thicker baking cups, where they may show through the cheaper ones. Metallic

gold, silver, and colored baking cups give good results and create a stunning effect for a special occasion. Baking cups also come in mini-muffin sizes. These may not be as easy to find but can be bought from mail-order cake decoration suppliers or online.

Baking Papers and Foil

Nonstick parchment paper is useful for lining the bases of small pans or for drying out chocolate and rolled fondant shapes. It is generally more versatile than wax (or 'waxed') paper. However, wax paper is useful for making triangular paper decorating bags. Parchment paper can also be used, but wax paper is better, as it is thinner and more flexible. A large sheet of aluminum foil is handy for wrapping your baked goods or for protecting wrapped cupcakes and muffins in the freezer.

Electric Mixers

A handheld electric mixer makes quick work of whisking butter and sugar and is an invaluable aid for baking, while a large stand mixer is useful if you are making larger quantities of cakes and frostings. Do not be tempted to use a food processor for mixing small amounts, because it is easy to overprocess and this may produce flat cakes.

Other Essential Items

In addition to the usual variety of mixing bowls, wooden spoons, measuring spoons, scissors, sieves, graters, skewers for testing cakes and wire racks for cooling, the following are particularly useful in cupcake-making.

Pastry Brush

A pastry brush is used for brushing glazes over cakes and melted butter around pans. Brushes tend to wear out regularly and shed their bristles, so keep a spare new brush handy.

Metal Spatulas

A small and a large metal spatula are ideal for many jobs, including loosening cakes from their pans, lifting cakes, and swirling on buttercream icing. A metal spatula with a cranked blade is useful for lifting small cakes or flat pieces of rolled fondant.

Stamps and Cookie Cutters

Stamps and cutters in almost any imaginable shape can be bought from specialist baking retailers. They come in classic metal cookie-cutter styles, in plastic, or plunger-style for embossing patterns. If you do not have appropriate cutters, you can use images found in books or magazines as templates.

Decorating Bags and Decorating Sets

A nylon decorating bag that comes with a decorating set of five or eight tips is a very useful piece of equipment for

decorating with icing. Look for a decorating set with a plain tip and various star tips for piping swirls around cupcakes. The larger the star tip, the wider the swirls will be on the finished cake. Disposable paper or clear plastic decorating bags are available, but nylon decorating bags can be washed out in warm soapy water and dried, ready to use again.

To Make a Paper Decorating Bag

Cut out a 15 x 10 inch rectangle of wax paper (or parchment paper). Fold it diagonally in half to form two triangular shapes. Cut along the fold line to make two triangles. One of these triangles can be used another time—it is quicker and easier to make two at a time from one square than to measure and mark out a triangle on a sheet of paper.

Fold one of the points on the long side of the triangle over the top to make a sharp cone and hold in the center. Fold the other sharp end of the triangle over the cone. Hold all the points together at the back of the cone, keeping the pointed end sharp. Turn the points inside the top edge, fold over to make a crease, then secure with a piece of adhesive tape. To use, snip off the end, place a piping tip in position, and fill the bag with icing. Or, fill the bag with icing first, then snip off a tiny hole at the end for piping a plain edge, writing, or piping tiny dots.

Ingredients

In cupcake-making, the classic cake base is made in the same way as any typical cake—that is, by mixing fats, sugar, flour and eggs together and varying with further ingredients or different methods to achieve the required result. Here is a selected outline of ingredients that are particularly useful or important in cupcake-making—which is mainly in the area of decorating!

Remember that when a recipe calls for 'softened' butter or margarine, it means *block* butter or margarine that has been removed from the refrigerator a little while before required—they are much easier to mix in when at room temperature.

Yogurt and Buttermilk

Plain yogurt adds richness and moisture to smaller cakes, and so is great for muffins. Do not use low-fat yogurt—stick to plain thick or Greek yogurt, which has more substance.

Adding bacteria to low-fat milk to thicken and sour it produces buttermilk. This is used in recipes for cupcakes and muffins that use baking soda because the acidity from the buttermilk produces carbon dioxide, which makes the mixture rise as it bakes. Buttermilk will give an extra lift to cupcakes and muffins, as well as a richer flavor. You will find buttermilk on sale in the dairy section of the supermarket but, as a substitute, you can add 1 tbsp lemon juice to 1¼ cups plain thick/Greek yogurt or whole milk.

Extracts

Flavoring extracts are very concentrated and usually sold in liquid form in small bottles. A teaspoon measure will usually be enough to flavor the mixture for 12 muffins. Vanilla and almond extracts are ideal for imparting their delicate flavors into mixtures and you will find the more expensive extracts give a finer, more natural flavor. Rosewater can be used for flavoring both mixtures and icings and has a delicate, perfumed flavor. Fruit flavorings, such as lemon, lime, orange, and raspberry, will give a fresh twist to mixtures and icings.

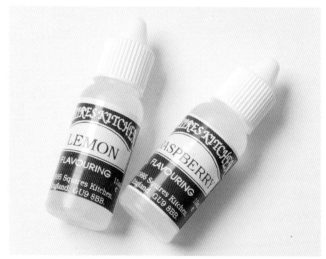

Chocolate

For the best results and a professional finish and flavor, it is always advisable to buy the highest quality of chocolate you can find, though this will be more expensive. Better-quality chocolates contain a higher percentage of real cocoa fat, which gives a flavor and texture far superior to cheaper varieties. (Cheaper chocolate contains a much smaller percentage of cocoa solids and is best avoided in favor of better-quality chocolate.) The amount of cocoa fat or solids contained in chocolate will be marked on the wrapper of any good-quality chocolate. Those marked as 70-percent cocoa solids will give the best results and you will find this chocolate is shiny and brittle and it should snap very easily.

Dark Chocolate
Dark or best-quality bittersweet chocolate with 70-percent cocoa solids is the most useful all-purpose type of chocolate for baking. It has a good strong flavour.

Semisweet Chocolate
Semisweet chocolate (also called milk chocolate) has sugar added and is sweeter than dark, so is good melted for icing and decorations.

White Chocolate
This is not strictly chocolate because it contains only cocoa butter, milk, and sugar. It is expensive and the most difficult to work with, so must be used with care. It is best to grate it finely. When melting it, keep the temperature very low.

Chocolate Cake Covering
This is a cheaper substitute containing a minimum of 2.5 percent cocoa solids and vegetable oil. It is considerably cheaper than real chocolate and the flavor is not as good, but it is easy to melt and sets quickly and well for a coating.

Chocolate Chips
Chocolate chips come in dark, milk, and white varieties. They are useful for adding to cupcake and muffin mixtures to enrich them and add a delicious texture because they only partly melt when baked.

Unsweetened Cocoa
To release its full flavor, unsweetened cocoa needs to be blended with boiling water into a paste and then cooled before adding to a recipe. It can also be sifted into the bowl with the flour.

Chocolate Flavored Drink Powder (or Cocoa Mix)
Be aware that this is not the same as unsweetened cocoa because it contains milk powder and sugar. Some recipes may specify using this and these are successful, but do not substitute it for unsweetened cocoa or it will spoil the flavor of a cake.

For Decorating

Powdered Sugar

Also known as confectioner's sugar, this is fine and powdery. It is usually sold plain and white, but can also be bought as an unrefined golden (or "natural") variety. Use it for delicate icing, frosting, and decorations. Store in a dry place because it can absorb moisture and this will make it go hard and lumpy. Always sift this sugar at least once, or preferably twice, before you use it, to remove any hard lumps that would prevent the icing from achieving a smooth texture—lumpy icing is impossible to pipe out.

Fondant Sugar, for Poured Fondant Icing

To be found also as "fondant and icing powdered sugar" or "poured fondant mix", this is sold in plain and flavored varieties and gives a beautiful glossy and professional finish to cake toppings. Just add a little boiled water, according to the package instructions, to make a shiny icing that can be poured over cupcakes. Color the icing with a few drops of paste food coloring to achieve your desired result. If you cannot find fondant sugar, powdered sugar can be used as a substitute; it just won't have that extra sheen.

Flavored fondant sugar is sold in a range of fruit flavors and also has coloring added. These sugars are ideal if you want to make a large batch of cakes with different colored and flavored toppings. They can also be whisked with softened unsalted butter and cream cheese to make delicious frostings in just a few moments.

Royal Icing Mix

Royal icing sets to a classic, firm Christmas-cake-style covering. This ready-mixed sugar is whisked with cold water to give an instant royal icing. Because it has dried egg white in the mixture, it does not need the long beating that traditional royal icing recipes require. It is also ideal to use for those who cannot eat raw egg whites.

Piping or Decorating Tubes

You can buy small tubes of colored royal icing or gel icing in a wide variety of colors. These are ideal for small amounts of writing or for piping on dots or small decorations.

Food Colorings

You can buy food colorings in the form of liquid, paste, gel, powder, or dust in a huge range of colors.

Dusts and sparkle colorings These should be lightly brushed onto dry rolled fondant to give a delicate sheen to decorations such as flowers.

Store-bought Sugar Decorations

A selection of pretty decorations, sprinkles and candies can be bought in supermarkets or online from specialist cake-decorating retailers. These provide a wonderful way to make quick and easy cake toppings.

Paste food colorings These are best for using with rolled fondant. They are sold in small tubs and are very concentrated, so should be added to the fondant dot by dot on the end of a wooden toothpick. Knead the coloring in evenly, adding more until you get the shade you require.

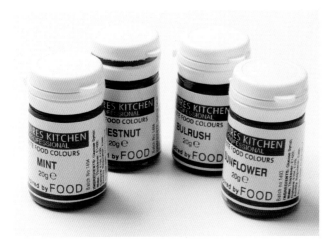

Liquid and gel food colorings Gel colorings are ideal for adding to frostings. Add this cautiously, drop by drop, beating the frosting well until you reach the color you require.

Basic Methods

Different Mixing Techniques

Creaming

The creaming method—which means that the butter and sugar are first beaten or "creamed" together—makes light cakes. A little care is needed for this method. Use a large mixing bowl to beat the fat and sugar together until pale and fluffy. The eggs are gradually beaten in to form a slackened batter and the flour is folded in last, to stiffen up the mixture.

Rubbing In

In this method, the fat is lightly worked into the flour between the fingers, as in pastry-making, until the mixture

resembles fine crumbs. This can be done by hand or in a food processor. Enough liquid is stirred in to give a soft mixture that will drop easily from a spoon. This method is often called for in recipes for pastry or easy fruitcakes.

All-In-One Mixtures

This "one-step" method is quick and easy—perfect for those new to baking—because it does not involve any complicated techniques. It is ideal for making light sponge cakes, but soft tub-type margarine or butter softened at room temperature must be used. There is no need for any creaming or rubbing

in because all the ingredients are simply placed in a large bowl and quickly beaten together for just a few minutes until smooth. Be careful not to overbeat—this will make the mixture too wet. Self-rising flour with the addition of a little extra baking powder is vital for a good rise.

The Melting Method

Cakes with a delicious moist, sticky texture, such as traditional gingerbread, are made by this method. These cakes use a high proportion of sugar and syrup, which are

gently warmed together in a saucepan with the fat, until the sugar granules have dissolved and the mixture is runny. It is important to cool the hot melted mixture a little before beating in flour, eggs, and spices to make the batter, or else the heat will damage the power of the leavening agent.

Checking to See if the Cakes Are Cooked

Cupcakes and muffins should be golden, risen, and firm to the touch when pressed lightly in the center. The last part of a cupcake or muffin to cook is the center, so, after the baking time stated, check this area. For light sponge cakes, press the center gently with your fingertips and, if the cake is cooked, it should spring back easily. To test more thoroughly,

insert a thin warmed skewer into the deepest part of the center. If the cake is cooked, it will come out perfectly clean with no mixture sticking to it but, if there is some on the skewer, bake the cakes for a little longer and test again.

Cooling the Cakes

All freshly baked cakes are very fragile; they need to stand in the pans to cool for a short time to make them firm. Sponge cakes and delicate cupcakes need standing time of about 2 minutes, muffins need 3–4 minutes, and fruity mixtures need 5 minutes.

If muffins start to stick to the pan, leave until they are firm, then loosen them by running a small metal spatula around their sides. Carefully turn the cakes out on a wire rack to cool. Do not leave cupcakes in paper baking cups in the cupcake pan to cool completely because moisture that collects in the pan will cause the paper baking cups to dampen and discolor.

How to Patch Up Mistakes

- If your cakes have peaked, trim them flat once they are cold (*see* right).

- If the cakes have overcooked or are burned on the outside, simply scrape this away with a serrated knife and cover the surface with buttercream.

- If the cakes are a little dry, sprinkle them with a few drops of sweet sherry or orange juice.

Cutting the Tops Level

Many cupcakes will form a small peak while baking and this is an ideal shape for coating with buttercream or piping a swirl of cream cheese icing around. However, some methods of decorating require a flat surface so, for these, trim the tops level with a sharp knife. Coat the cupcakes with apricot glaze and press on a disk of almond paste or rolled fondant to give you a flat surface to decorate.

Storing Cupcakes

- Make sure cupcakes or muffins are completely cold before storing, otherwise condensation can form in the container, which can cause the cakes to turn moldy.

- Large, shallow plastic food containers with airtight lids are ideal for cupcakes and muffins because they enable the cakes to be kept flat in one single layer and even small cupcakes will stay moist. Old-fashioned cake tins may be used, but they do not hold a large number of small cakes. If you do not have a cake tin or container that is big enough, invert a large mixing bowl over the cupcakes on a plate or flat surface and this will keep them fresh.

- Cupcakes made from sponge cake will keep for 3–4 days, and richer fruit cupcakes for 5 days to a week. Cakes with fresh cream fillings and decorations need to be kept in the refrigerator and are best eaten on the day of filling with cream.

- Store cakes with fondant decorations in a cool place, but *not* in the refrigerator. The moisture in a refrigerator will be absorbed by the fondant and the icing will go limp and soggy.

Freezing Cupcakes

Most cupcakes will freeze well but, for best results, freeze undecorated. Completely cool each cake and freeze in one layer on a cookie sheet or baking pan. Once frozen, place in strong freezer bags or boxes, and seal to exclude as much air as possible, label, and freeze. Cakes containing fresh fruits such as blueberries or raspberries will not freeze well, because the fruit tends to make the cakes soggy when thawed, so these are best eaten fresh on the day of baking.

To use frozen cakes, completely unwrap and thaw at room temperature on racks. The paper baking cups may peel away from frozen cakes, so these may need to be replaced with fresh ones before decorating the cakes.

Basic Cake Recipes

Basic Vanilla Cupcakes

**Makes 18 cupcakes
or 36 mini cupcakes**

1 cup butter, softened
1 cup superfine sugar
4 large eggs, beaten
2 cups self-rising flour
½ tsp baking powder
2 tbsp low-fat milk
1 tsp vanilla extract
1 tsp glycerin

Preheat the oven to 350°F and line appropriate pans with
the correct number of paper baking cups. Whisk the butter
and sugar together, preferably with an electric hand mixer,
until pale and fluffy. Whisk in the eggs gradually, adding a
teaspoon of flour with each addition to prevent the mixture
from curdling.

Sift the remaining flour and baking powder into the bowl, then
gradually whisk in the milk, extract, and glycerin. Spoon the
mixture into the paper baking cups and bake for 25 minutes
for the cupcakes or 12 minutes for the mini cupcakes, or until
firm and golden. Cool on a wire rack. Keep for 3–4 days in an
airtight container.

Mini Cupcakes

Makes about 24

⅓ cup unrefined superfine sugar
scant ½ cup butter, softened

finely grated zest and juice of ½ lemon
2 large eggs, beaten
¾ cup self-rising flour
2 tsp milk

Preheat the oven to 375°F. Grease a mini-muffin pan or line
it with mini-muffin-sized paper baking cups. Put the sugar,
butter, and lemon zest in a large bowl and beat until light
and fluffy. Add the beaten eggs a little at a time, adding a
teaspoon of flour with each addition. Fold in the flour,
lemon juice, and milk and mix until smooth.

Spoon the batter into the prepared pan or baking cups.
Bake for about 12 minutes until golden and risen.
Transfer to a wire rack to cool. Keep for 2–3 days in an
airtight container.

Quick All-in-One Mix for Cupcakes

Makes 12 cupcakes

½ cup superfine sugar
½ cup soft tub margarine
2 large eggs
1 cup self-rising flour
1 tsp milk or lemon juice

Preheat the oven to 375°F. Line a muffin pan with 12 paper baking cups. Place all the cake ingredients in a large bowl and beat with an electric mixer for about 2 minutes until smooth. Half-fill the paper baking cups with the mixture. Bake for about 15 minutes until firm, risen and golden. Remove to a wire rack to cool. Keep for 2–3 days in an airtight container.

Individual Fruitcakes

Makes 12 cupcakes

½ cup butter
1¼ cups soft dark muscovado sugar
2 large eggs, beaten

2 cups self-rising flour
1 tsp ground pumpkin pie spice
finely grated zest, and 1 tbsp juice, of 1 orange
1 tbsp molasses
2¼ cups mixed dried fruit

Preheat the oven to 350°F. Line muffin pans with 12 paper baking cups. Beat the butter and sugar together until light and fluffy, then beat in the eggs a little at a time, adding a teaspoon of flour with each addition. Sift in the remaining flour and pumpkin pie spice, add the orange zest and juice, molasses, and dried fruit to the bowl and fold together until the mixture is blended.

Spoon into the baking cups and bake for 30–35 minutes until firm in the center and a skewer comes out clean. Leave to cool in the pans for 15 minutes, then turn out to cool on a wire rack. Store in an airtight container for up to 4 weeks, or freeze until needed.

Chocolate Fudge Cupcakes

**Makes 12 cupcakes
or 22 mini cupcakes**

⅔ cup butter, softened
⅔ cup golden superfine sugar
3 large eggs, beaten
1 cup self-rising flour
¼ cup unsweetened cocoa
1 tbsp milk

Preheat the oven to 375°F. Line appropriate pans with enough foil or paper baking cups. Place the butter, superfine sugar, and eggs in a large bowl and then sift in the flour and unsweetened cocoa. Whisk together with the milk until smooth for about 2 minutes, then spoon into the baking cups, filling them two-thirds full.

Bake for about 20 minutes for the cupcakes or 12–14 minutes for the mini cupcakes until well risen and springy to the touch. Cool on a wire rack. Keep for up to 3 days in an airtight container.

Carrot Cupcakes

**Makes 12 cupcakes
or 22 mini cupcakes**

1½ cups carrots, peeled
1¼ cups self-rising whole-wheat flour
1 tsp baking powder
½ tsp ground cinnamon
pinch salt
⅔ cup corn oil or canola oil
⅔ cup soft light brown sugar
3 large eggs, beaten
1 tsp vanilla extract
½ cup raisins or golden raisins

Preheat the oven to 350°F. Lightly oil or line appropriate pans with enough paper baking cups. Grate the carrots finely. Sift the flour, baking powder, cinnamon, and salt into a bowl, then tip in any wheat germ from the sieve. Add the oil, sugar, eggs, extract, golden raisins, and grated carrots.

Beat until smooth, then spoon into the prepared pan or cups. Bake for 25 minutes for the cupcakes or 15–20 minutes for the mini cupcakes until risen and golden. Cool on a wire rack. Keep for up to 5 days in an airtight container.

Basic Icing Recipes

Cream Cheese Frosting

Covers 12 cupcakes

¼ cup unsalted butter, softened
1⅓ cups powdered sugar, sifted
flavorings of choice
food colorings of choice
½ cup full-fat cream cheese

Beat the butter and powdered sugar together until light and fluffy. Add flavorings and colorings of choice and beat again. Add the cream cheese and whisk until light and fluffy. Do not overbeat, however, because the mixture can become runny.

Basic Buttercream Frosting

Covers 12 cupcakes

¼ cup unsalted butter, softened
1¾ cups powdered sugar, sifted
2 tbsp hot milk or water
1 tsp vanilla extract
food colorings of choice

Beat the butter until light and fluffy, then beat in half the sifted powdered sugar and half the hot milk or water, then beat in the remaining powdered sugar and milk or water. Add the vanilla extract and any food colorings. Store chilled for up to 2 days in a lidded container.

Chocolate Fudge Icing

Covers 12 cupcakes

4 oz dark chocolate, broken into pieces
¼ cup unsalted butter

whisk in the egg with the powdered sugar and vanilla extract. Whisk until smooth and glossy, then use immediately or leave to cool and thicken for a spreading consistency.

Royal Icing

Makes 1 lb (or enough to cover 12 deep cupcakes)

2 medium egg whites
4 cups powdered sugar, sifted
2 tsp lemon juice

Put the egg whites in a large bowl and whisk lightly with a fork until foamy. Sift in half the powdered sugar with the lemon juice and beat well with an electric mixer for 4 minutes, or by hand with a wooden spoon for about 10 minutes, until smooth.

Gradually sift in the remaining powdered sugar and beat again until thick, smooth, and brilliant white and the icing

1 large egg, beaten
1⅓ cups unrefined powdered sugar, sifted
½ tsp vanilla extract

Place the chocolate and butter in a bowl over a pan of hot water and stir until melted. Remove from the heat and

forms soft peaks when flicked up with a spoon. Keep the royal icing covered with a clean damp cloth until you are ready to use it, or store in the refrigerator in a plastic container with an airtight lid until needed. If making royal icing ahead of time to use later, beat it again before use to remove any air bubbles that may have formed in the mixture.

Tip For a softer royal icing that will not set too hard, beat 1 tsp glycerin into the mixture.

Glacé Icing

Covers 12 cupcakes

1¾ cups powdered sugar
few drops lemon juice or vanilla or almond extract
2–3 tbsp boiling water
liquid food coloring (optional)

Sift the powdered sugar into a bowl and add the chosen flavoring. Gradually stir in enough boiling water to mix to the consistency of thick cream. Beat with a wooden spoon until thick enough to coat the back of the spoon. Add coloring, if liked. Use at once because the icing will begin to form a skin.

Apricot Glaze

Makes 1 lb (or enough to cover 24 cupcakes)

1½ cups apricot jam
3 tbsp water
1 tsp lemon juice

Place the jam, water and juice in a heavy-based saucepan and heat gently, stirring, until soft and melted. Boil rapidly for 1 minute, then press through a fine sieve with the back of a wooden spoon. Discard the pieces of fruit. Use immediately for glazing or sticking on almond paste, or pour into a clean jar or plastic lidded container and refrigerate for up to 3 months.

Almond Paste

Makes 1 lb (or enough to cover 24 cupcakes)

1 cup powdered sugar, sifted
½ cup superfine sugar
1¼ cups ground almonds
1 large egg
1 tsp lemon juice

Stir the sugars and ground almonds together in a bowl. Whisk the egg and lemon juice together and mix into the dry ingredients.

Knead until the paste is smooth. Wrap tightly in plastic wrap or foil to keep airtight and store in the refrigerator until needed. The paste can be made 2–3 days ahead of time but, after that, it will start to dry out and become difficult to handle.

To use the almond paste, knead on a surface lightly dusted with powdered sugar until soft and pliable. Brush the top of each cake with apricot glaze. Roll out the almond paste and cut out disks large enough to cover the tops of the cakes. Press onto the cakes.

Ready-to-roll Fondant Icing

Makes 12 oz (or enough cover 12 cupcakes or to use for decorations)

1 large egg white
1 tbsp liquid glucose (or corn syrup, if you can't find glucose)
2¾ cups powdered sugar, sifted

Place the egg white and liquid glucose or corn syrup in a large mixing bowl and stir together with a fork, breaking up the egg white. Add the powdered sugar gradually, mixing in with a metal spatula, until the mixture binds together and forms a ball. Turn the ball of icing out onto a clean surface dusted with powdered sugar and knead for 5 minutes until soft but firm enough to roll out. If the icing is too soft, knead in a little more powdered sugar until the mixture is pliable.

To color, knead in paste food coloring. Do not use liquid food coloring—it is not suitable and will make the fondant go limp.

To use, roll out thinly on a clean surface dusted with powdered sugar and cut out disks large enough to cover the top of each cake. Brush the almond paste (if using as a layer underneath the rolled fondant disks) with a little boiled water that has been allowed to cool, or some clear liquor such as kirsch, and press onto the cake, then press the rolled fondant on top of the almond paste topping. Alternatively, coat the cakes with a little buttercream, place the rolled fondant disk on top and press down.

To mold, knead lightly and roll out thinly on a surface dusted with powdered sugar. Use cutters or templates (*see* Making Flat Decorations, pages 37–38) to make flowers or shapes. Mold into shapes with your fingertips and leave to dry out for 24 hours in egg cartons lined with plastic wrap.

Decorating Techniques and Tips

Using Chocolate

Melting Chocolate

Care and attention is needed to melt chocolate for baking and decorating muffins and cupcakes. If the chocolate gets too hot or comes into contact with water or steam, it will "seize" or stiffen and form into a hard ball instead of a smooth melted mixture. You can add a little vegetable oil or margarine, a teaspoon at a time, to the mixture to make it liquid again.

To melt chocolate, break the bar into small pieces, or grate or chop it, and place in a heatproof bowl standing over a bowl of warm, not hot, water. Make sure the bowl containing the chocolate is completely dry and that steam or water cannot enter the bowl. Heat the water to a gentle simmer only and leave the bowl to stand for about 5 minutes. Do not let the water get too hot or the chocolate will reach too high a temperature and will lose its sheen.

The microwave oven is ideal for melting chocolate. Place the chocolate pieces in a small microwave-proof bowl and melt gently on low or defrost settings in small bursts of 30 seconds, checking and stirring in between, until the chocolate has melted.

Making Chocolate Decorations

Curls and shavings Spread melted chocolate out thinly onto a clean dry surface such as a plastic or marble board or a clean worktop. Leave the chocolate until almost set, then pull a long sharp-bladed knife through it at an angle to form curls or shavings. Place the curls sealed in a plastic box with an airtight lid in the refrigerator until needed for decoration.

Leaves Wash and dry holly or rose leaves and place on a sheet of nonstick parchment paper. Melt the chocolate and paint on the underside of each leaf. Leave to dry out, then

carefully peel away the leaf. You will find the veined side is uppermost on the chocolate leaf. Place in a lidded container and keep refrigerated until needed for decoration.

Crystallizing Petals, Flowers, Leaves, and Berries

Make sure you only use edible plants! Wash and dry herbs and leaves such as rosemary sprigs and small bay leaves or berries such as cranberries. Separate edible petals from small flowers such as rosebuds and clean small flowers such as violets with a clean brush, but do not wash them.

Beat 1 large egg white with 2 tsp cold water until frothy. Paint a thin layer of egg white carefully over the items, then sprinkle lightly with superfine sugar, shaking to remove any excess. Leave to dry on a wire rack lined with nonstick parchment paper.

Using Buttercream and Cream Cheese Frostings

These soft icings can be swirled onto the tops of cupcakes with a small metal spatula or placed in a decorating bag fitted with a star tip to pipe impressive whirls.

- Do not be stingy with the amount of frosting you use. If this is scraped on thinly, you will see the cake underneath, so be generous.

- Keep cupcakes with frostings in a cool place, or refrigerate—as they contain a high percentage of butter, which will melt easily in too warm a place.

- Cupcakes coated in buttercream can be decorated easily with colorful sprinkles and coarse colored sugars. To make this easy, place the sprinkles in a small saucer or on a piece of nonstick parchment paper and roll the outside edges of each cupcake in the decorations.

Using Ready-to-roll Fondant

Fondant is a versatile icing because it can be used for covering cupcakes or modeling all sorts of fancy decorations. To use as a covering, roll out the fondant thinly on a surface dusted with powdered sugar and cut out circles the size of the cake tops. Coat each cake with a little apricot glaze or buttercream and press on the circles to form a flat surface.

Making Flat Decorations

To make letters, numbers, or flat decorations, roll out the fondant thinly and cut out the shapes freehand or with

Decorating Tips

- Always roll out almond paste or fondant icing on a surface lightly dusted with powdered sugar.

- Leave fondant-covered cakes to firm up for 2 hours before adding decorations. This provides a good finished surface to work on.

- Tie ribbons around the finished cupcake and secure them with a dab of royal icing. Never use pins in ribbons on a cake.

- Once decorated, store fondant-covered cakes in large boxes in a cool place. Do not store in a refrigerator, because the fondant will become damp and the colors may run.

- Paste food colorings are best for working with fondant and a little goes a very long way. These are very concentrated, so use a wooden toothpick to add dots of paste gradually until you are sure of the color and then knead in until even.

cutters. You may have some templates or images that you would like to replicate, in which case, trace the pattern you want onto a sheet of clear wax paper or nonstick parchment paper, then position the paper over the fondant. Mark over the pattern with the tip of a small sharp knife or a pin. Remove the paper and cut out the marked-on pattern with a small sharp knife. Leave to dry on nonstick parchment paper on a flat surface or a cookie sheet for 2–3 hours to make them firm and easy to handle.

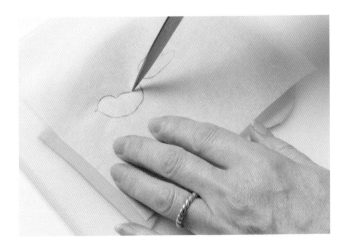

Delectable Delights

Mini Carrot Cupcakes

Makes 22

1½ cups self-rising whole-wheat flour
1 tsp baking powder
½ tsp ground cinnamon
pinch salt
⅔ cup corn oil or canola oil
⅔ cup soft light brown sugar
3 large eggs, beaten
1 tsp vanilla extract
½ cup golden raisins
1½ cups peeled and grated carrots

To decorate:
1 orange
heaping ¼ cup cream cheese
1⅓ cups powdered sugar (golden, if possible)

1. Preheat the oven to 350°F. Lightly oil 22 holes in a mini-muffin pan(s).

2. Sift the flour, baking powder, cinnamon, and salt into a bowl, along with any wheat germ from the sieve.

3. Add the oil, sugar, eggs, vanilla extract, golden raisins, and grated carrots. Beat until smooth, then spoon into the prepared pans. Bake for about 20 minutes until risen and golden. Cool on a wire rack.

4. To decorate, peel thin strips of zest from the orange. Beat the cream cheese and powdered sugar together with 2 tsp juice from the orange to make a spreading consistency. Swirl the icing over each cupcake and then top with shreds of orange zest. Keep for up to 3 days in an airtight container in a cool place.

Shaggy Coconut Cupcakes

Makes 12

½ tsp baking powder
1⅔ cups self-rising flour
¾ cup superfine sugar
2 tbsp dried shredded coconut
¾ cup soft tub margarine
3 large eggs, beaten
2 tbsp milk

To decorate:
1 batch buttercream
  (*see* page 29)
1 tbsp coconut liqueur
  (optional)
2 cups large shredded
  coconut strands

1. Preheat the oven to 350°F. Line a muffin pan with 12 paper baking cups.

2. Sift the baking powder and flour into a large bowl. Add all the remaining ingredients and beat for about 2 minutes until smooth and creamy. Divide evenly between the paper baking cups.

3. Bake for 18–20 minutes until risen, golden, and firm to the touch. Leave in the muffin pans for 2 minutes, then turn out to cool on a wire rack.

4. To decorate the cupcakes, beat the coconut liqueur (if using) into the buttercream and then swirl the buttercream over each cupcake. Press large strands of shredded coconut into the buttercream. Keep for up to 3 days in an airtight container in a cool place.

Coffee & Walnut Fudge Cupcakes

Makes 16–18

1 cup self-rising flour
½ cup (8 tbsp) butter, softened
½ cup superfine sugar (golden, if possible)
2 large eggs, beaten
1 tbsp golden syrup (or corn syrup)
½ cup walnuts, finely chopped

To decorate:
1¾ cups golden powdered sugar
½ cup (8 tbsp) unsalted butter, softened
2 tsp coffee extract
16–18 small walnut pieces

1. Preheat the oven to 400°F. Line muffin pans with 16–18 foil baking cups, depending on the depth of the cups.

2. Stir the flour into a bowl and add the butter, sugar, eggs, and syrup. Beat for about 2 minutes, then fold in the walnuts.

3. Spoon the mixture into the foil baking cups and bake for about 12–14 minutes until well risen and springy in the center. Remove to a wire rack to cool.

4. Make the frosting by sifting the powdered sugar into a bowl. Add the butter, coffee extract, and 1 tbsp hot water. Beat until light and fluffy, then place in a decorating bag fitted with a star tip. Pipe a swirl on each cupcake and top with a walnut piece. Keep for 3–4 days in an airtight container in a cool place.

Mini Cupcakes

Makes 24

⅓ cup superfine sugar
  (golden, if possible)
scant ½ cup (7 tbsp)
  butter, softened
finely grated zest of
  ½ lemon and 1 tsp juice
2 large eggs, beaten
¾ cup self-rising flour

To decorate:
¼ cup unsalted
  butter, softened
1 tsp vanilla extract
1 cup powdered sugar, sifted
1 tbsp milk
paste food colorings
sugar sprinkles

1. Preheat the oven to 375°F. Line a mini-muffin pan with 24 mini-muffin paper baking cups.

2. Put the sugar, butter, and lemon zest in a large bowl and beat until light and fluffy. Beat in the eggs a little at a time, adding a teaspoon of flour with each addition. Fold in the rest of the flour and the lemon juice and mix until smooth.

3. Spoon into the baking cups and bake for about 12 minutes until golden and risen. Transfer to a wire rack to cool.

4. To make the icing, beat the butter and vanilla extract together until light and fluffy, then gradually beat in the powdered sugar and milk until a soft, easy-to-spread consistency has formed. Color the icing in batches with paste food coloring, then spread over the cold cupcakes with a flat-bladed knife. Decorate with sugar sprinkles. Keep in an airtight container for up to 2 days.

Banoffee Cupcakes

Makes 10–12

1 soft, ripe extra large banana,
  about 9–10 inches long
½ cup soft tub margarine
⅓ cup superfine sugar (golden,
  if possible)
1 tbsp milk
2 large eggs
1¾ cups all-purpose flour
1 tbsp baking powder
3 oz mini soft fudge pieces

To decorate:
1 cup powdered
  sugar (golden, if
  possible)
10–12 semi-dried
  banana flakes

1. Preheat the oven to 350°F. Line a muffin pan with 10–12 paper baking cups, depending on the depth of the cups.

2. Peel and mash the banana in a large bowl, then add the margarine, sugar, milk, and eggs. Sift in the flour and baking powder and beat together for about 2 minutes until smooth.

3. Fold in two thirds of the fudge pieces and then spoon the mixture into the baking cups. Bake for about 20 minutes until golden and firm. Remove from the muffin pans to a wire rack to cool.

4. For the decoration, blend the powdered sugar with 3–4 tsp cold water to make a thin icing. Drizzle over the top of each cupcake and, while the icing is still wet, top with the remaining mini fudge pieces and the banana flakes. Leave to dry out for 30 minutes to set the icing. Keep in an airtight container for up to 3 days.

Strawberry Swirl Cupcakes

Makes 12

½ cup superfine sugar	**To decorate:**
½ cup soft tub margarine	¼ cup (4 tbsp) unsalted
2 large eggs	butter, softened
1 cup self-rising flour	1⅓ cups powdered
½ tsp baking powder	sugar, sifted
2 tbsp sieved	½ cup full-fat cream cheese
strawberry jam	1 tbsp sieved strawberry jam
	pink food coloring

1. Preheat the oven to 375°F. Line a muffin pan with 12 paper baking cups.

2. Place all the cupcake ingredients except the jam in a large bowl and beat with an electric mixer for about 2 minutes until smooth. Fill the baking cups halfway up with the mixture.

3. Add ½ teaspoon jam to each baking cup and swirl it into the mixture. Bake for about 15 minutes until firm, risen, and golden. Remove to a wire rack to cool.

4. To prepare the frosting, beat the butter until soft, then gradually add the powdered sugar until the mixture is light. Add the cream cheese and whisk until light and fluffy.

5. Divide the mixture in half and beat the strawberry jam and pink food coloring into one half. Fit a decorating bag with a wide star tip and spoon strawberry cream on one side of the bag and the plain cream on the other. Pipe swirls on top of the cupcakes. Keep for up to 3 days in an airtight container in a cool place.

Double Cherry Cupcakes

Makes 12

¼ cup candied cherries, washed,
  dried, and chopped
1 cup self-rising flour
¼ cup dried sour cherries
½ cup soft tub margarine
½ cup superfine sugar
2 large eggs
½ tsp almond extract

To decorate:
1¼ cup fondant sugar or
  powdered sugar
pale pink liquid food coloring
2 tbsp candied cherries

1. Preheat the oven to 375°F. Line a muffin pan with
   12 paper baking cups.

2. Dust the chopped candied cherries lightly in 1 tbsp of the
   flour, then mix with the sour cherries and set aside. Sift the
   rest of the flour into a bowl, then add the margarine, sugar,
   eggs, and almond extract. Beat for about 2 minutes until
   smooth, then fold in the cherries.

3. Spoon the batter into the baking cups and bake for 15–20
   minutes until well risen and springy in the center. Turn out
   to cool on a wire rack.

4. To decorate the cupcakes, trim the tops level. Mix the
   powdered sugar with 2–3 tsp warm water and a
   few drops of pink food coloring to make a thick
   consistency. Spoon the icing over each cupcake, filling
   right up to the edge.

5. Chop the cherries finely and sprinkle over the icing.
   Leave to set for 30 minutes. Keep for up to 3 days in an
   airtight container.

Ginger & Lemon Cupcakes

Makes 18

½ cup golden syrup
  (or corn syrup)
½ cup (8 tbsp) block margarine
1¾ cups all-purpose flour
2 tsp ground ginger
⅔ cup golden raisins
¼ cup soft dark brown sugar
1 cup milk
1 tsp baking soda
1 large egg, beaten

To decorate:
1 cup golden
powdered sugar
1 tsp lemon juice
candied ginger pieces

1. Preheat the oven to 350°F. Line muffin pans with 18 paper baking cups.

2. Place the syrup and margarine in a heavy-based saucepan and melt together gently. Sift the flour and ginger into a bowl, then stir in the golden raisins and sugar. Warm the milk and stir in the baking soda.

3. Pour the syrup mixture, milk, and beaten egg into the dry ingredients and beat until smooth. Pour the batter into a pitcher or large liquid measuring cup.

4. Carefully spoon 2 tbsp of the batter into each baking cup (it will be very wet and runny). Bake for about 30 minutes. Cool in the pans for 10 minutes, then turn out to cool on a wire rack.

5. To decorate, blend the powdered sugar with the lemon juice and 1 tbsp warm water to make a thin glacé icing. Drizzle over the top of each cupcake, then top with candied ginger pieces. Leave to set for 30 minutes. Keep in an airtight container for up to 5 days.

Crystallized Violet Cupcakes

Makes 12

²/₃ cup butter (1¼ sticks), softened
²/₃ cup superfine sugar
3 large eggs, beaten
1¼ cups self-rising flour
½ tsp baking powder
1 lemon

To decorate:
12 fresh violets
1 egg white
superfine sugar, for dusting
1 cup fondant sugar or powdered sugar
pale violet food coloring

1. Preheat the oven to 350°F and line a muffin pan with 12 paper baking cups.

2. Place the butter, sugar, and eggs in a bowl. Sift in the flour and baking powder. Finely grate in the zest from the lemon.

3. Beat together for about 2 minutes with an electric hand mixer until pale and fluffy. Spoon into the baking cups and bake for 20–25 minutes until firm and golden. Cool on a wire rack.

4. To decorate the cupcakes, spread the violets on some nonstick parchment paper. Beat the egg white until frothy, then brush thinly over the violets. Dust with superfine sugar and leave to dry out for 2 hours.

5. Beat the fondant sugar or powdered sugar with the coloring and enough water to give a thin coating consistency. Drizzle over the top of each cupcake quickly and top with a violet. Leave to set for 30 minutes. Store in an airtight container in a cool place. Keep for up to 2 days.

Daisy Chain Lemon Cupcakes

Makes 12

½ cup superfine sugar	**To decorate:**
½ cup soft tub margarine	2 oz rolled fondant
2 large eggs	yellow piping icing tube
1 cup self-rising flour	1¾ cups fondant sugar or
½ tsp baking powder	powdered sugar
1 tsp lemon juice	lemon yellow food coloring

1. Preheat the oven to 375°F. Line a muffin pan with 12 paper baking cups.

2. Place all the cupcake ingredients in a large bowl and beat with an electric mixer for about 2 minutes until smooth. Fill the baking cups halfway up with the batter.

3. Bake for 15 minutes until firm, risen, and golden. Remove to a wire rack to cool.

4. Roll out the fondant thinly and stamp out small daisies with a fluted daisy cutter. Pipe a small yellow dot of icing into the center of each and leave to dry out for 1 hour.

5. Blend the fondant sugar or powdered sugar with a little water and a few dots of yellow coloring to make a thick easy-to-spread icing, then smooth over the top of each cupcake. Decorate with the cut-out daisies immediately and leave to set for 1 hour. Keep for up to 3 days in an airtight container.

Florentine-topped Cupcakes

Makes 18

²/₃ cup butter (1¼ sticks), softened
²/₃ cup superfine sugar
1½ cups self-rising flour
3 large eggs
1 tsp vanilla extract
⅓ cup candied cherries, chopped
¼ cup angelica, chopped
¼ cup candied peel, chopped
⅓ cup dried cranberries

To decorate:
3 oz dark or semisweet
  chocolate, melted
½ cup flaked almonds

1. Preheat the oven to 350°F. Line muffin pans with 18 paper baking cups.

2. Place the butter and sugar in a bowl, then sift in the flour. In another bowl, beat the eggs with the vanilla extract, then add to the first mixture and beat until smooth.

3. Fold in half the cherries, angelica, peel, and cranberries. Spoon into the baking cups, filling them three-quarters full.

4. Bake for about 18 minutes until firm to the touch in the center. Turn out to cool on a wire rack.

5. Spoon a little melted chocolate on top of each cupcake, then scatter the remaining cherries, angelica, peel, cranberries and the almonds into the wet chocolate. Drizzle the remaining chocolate over the fruit topping with a teaspoon and leave to set for 30 minutes. Keep for up to 2 days in an airtight container.

Fondant Fancies

Makes 16–18

1¼ cups self-rising flour
²⁄₃ cup superfine sugar
½ cup ground almonds
²⁄₃ cup butter (1¼ sticks),
  softened
3 large eggs, beaten
4 tbsp milk

To decorate:
3¼ cups fondant sugar
  or powdered sugar
paste food colorings
selection fancy cake
  decorations

1. Preheat the oven to 350°F. Line muffin pans with
   16–18 paper baking cups, depending on the depth of
   the cups.

2. Sift the flour into a bowl and stir in the superfine sugar
   and almonds. Add the butter, eggs, and milk and beat
   until smooth.

3. Spoon into the paper cups and bake for 15–20 minutes
   until golden and firm to the touch. Turn out to cool on a
   wire rack. When cool, trim the tops flat if they have
   peaked slightly.

4. To decorate the cupcakes, make the poured fondant icing
   to a thick coating consistency, following the packet
   instructions. Divide into batches and color each separately
   with a little paste food coloring. Keep each bowl covered
   with a damp cloth until needed. Spoon some icing over
   each cupcake, being sure to flood it right to the edge.
   Top each with a fancy decoration and leave to set for
   30 minutes. Keep for up to 2 days in a cool place.

Lemon & Cardamom Cupcakes with Mascarpone Topping

Makes 12

1 tsp cardamom seeds
1 cup (2 sticks) butter
½ cup all-purpose flour
1⅔ cups self-rising flour
1 tsp baking powder
heaping ¼ cup superfine sugar
zest of 1 lemon, finely grated
3 large eggs
½ cup natural yogurt
4 tbsp lemon curd

To decorate:
1 heaping cup
   mascarpone cheese
heaping ⅓ cup powdered sugar
1 tsp lemon juice
lemon zest strips

1. Preheat the oven to 350°F. Line a muffin pan with 12 paper baking cups. Crush the cardamom seeds and remove the outer shells. Melt the butter and leave aside to cool.

2. Sift the flours and baking powder into a bowl and stir in the crushed seeds, sugar, and lemon zest.

3. In another bowl, whisk together the eggs and yogurt. Pour into the dry ingredients with the cooled melted butter and beat until combined.

4. Divide half the mixture between the baking cups, put a teaspoon of lemon curd into each, then top with the remaining mixture. Bake for about 25 minutes until golden.

5. To make the topping, beat the mascarpone with the powdered sugar and lemon juice. Swirl onto each cupcake and top with lemon strips. Eat fresh on the day of baking once decorated, or store undecorated in an airtight container for up to 2 days and add the topping just before serving.

Chocolate
Indulgence

Chocolate Mud Cupcakes

Makes 16

⅔ cup (1¼ sticks)
  butter, softened
⅔ cup superfine sugar
  (golden, if possible)
3 large eggs, beaten
1 cup self-rising flour
¼ cup unsweetened cocoa

To decorate:
3 oz semisweet chocolate
⅓ cup (6 tbsp) unsalted
  butter, softened
1¼ cups powdered sugar
  (golden, if possible), sifted
white and dark
  chocolate sprinkles

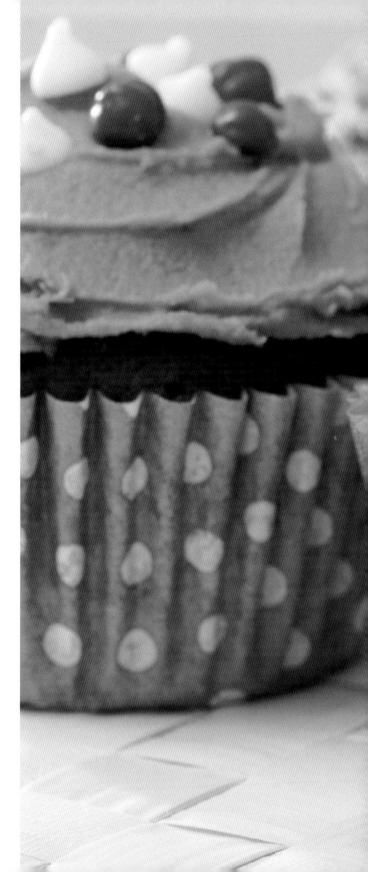

1. Preheat the oven to 375°F. Line muffin pans with 16 foil or paper baking cups.

2. Place the butter, superfine sugar, and eggs in a large bowl and then sift in the flour and unsweetened cocoa. Whisk together for about 2 minutes until smooth, then spoon into the baking cups, filling them two-thirds full.

3. Bake for about 14 minutes until well risen and springy to the touch. Cool on a wire rack.

4. To make the frosting, break the chocolate into squares and melt in a heatproof bowl over a pan of barely simmering water. Set aside to cool. Beat the butter and sugar together until fluffy, then whisk in the cooled melted chocolate. Swirl over the cupcakes with a flat-bladed knife. Scatter over the sprinkles. Keep for up to 3 days in a cool place.

White Chocolate Cupcakes

Makes 12

1 cup (2 sticks) butter
4 oz white chocolate
½ cup all-purpose flour
1⅔ cups self-rising flour
1 tsp baking powder
heaping ¾ cup superfine sugar
finely grated zest of ½ lemon
3 large eggs
½ cup plain Greek yogurt
2 cups chopped white chocolate

1. Preheat the oven to 350°F. Line a muffin pan with 12 paper baking cups. Melt the butter and leave aside to cool.

2. Coarsely grate or chop the white chocolate. Sift the flours and baking powder into a bowl and stir in the sugar, lemon zest, and chopped white chocolate.

3. In another bowl, whisk together the eggs and yogurt. Pour into the dry ingredients with the cooled melted butter and beat until combined. Spoon into the baking cups and bake for about 25 minutes until firm and golden.

4. To decorate the cupcakes, melt one quarter of the white chocolate in a heatproof bowl standing over a pan of barely simmering water. Spread the melted chocolate out onto a clean plastic board. When almost set, make into curls by pulling a sharp knife through the chocolate (*see* page 35). Refrigerate for 30 minutes to set.

5. Melt the remaining white chocolate, then spoon over the cupcakes and leave for about 10 minutes until cooled and half set. Top each cupcake while still wet with the white chocolate curls and leave to set for 30 minutes. Keep for up to 2 days in the refrigerator.

Double Chocolate Chip Cupcakes

Makes 14

½ cup soft tub margarine
½ cup superfine sugar (golden, if possible)
2 large eggs, beaten
¼ cup unsweetened cocoa
1½ cups self-rising flour
1 tsp baking powder
⅓ cup semisweet chocolate chips
⅓ cup dark or white chocolate chips
1 tbsp milk

1. Preheat the oven to 350°F. Line muffin pans with 14 paper baking cups.

2. Place the margarine and sugar in a large bowl with the eggs and sift in the unsweetened cocoa, flour, and baking powder. Beat for about 2 minutes until smooth, then fold in the chocolate chips with the milk.

3. Spoon into the baking cups and bake for 15–20 minutes until firm. Place on a wire rack to cool. Keep for 4–5 days in an airtight container

Chocolate Fudge Flake Cupcakes

Makes 12

1 cup self-rising flour
¼ cup unsweetened cocoa
½ cup soft tub margarine
⅔ cup soft light brown sugar
2 large eggs, beaten
2 tbsp milk

To decorate:
2 tbsp butter
2 tbsp golden syrup (or corn syrup)
2 tbsp unsweetened cocoa
1 cup powdered sugar (golden, if possible)
2 tbsp cream cheese
1½ oz chocolate flake bars or other chocolate candies

1. Preheat the oven to 350°F. Line a muffin pan with 12 paper baking cups.

2. Sift the flour and unsweetened cocoa into a large bowl, add the margarine, sugar, eggs, and milk and whisk with an electric beater for about 2 minutes until smooth.

3. Divide the mixture between the baking cups and bake for about 20 minutes for the large cupcakes and 15 minutes for the small cupcakes until a skewer inserted into the middle comes out clean. Turn out to cool on a wire rack.

4. To make the topping, melt the butter with the syrup and unsweetened cocoa in a pan. Cool, then whisk in the powdered sugar until the mixture has thickened, and beat in the cream cheese. Spread the frosting over the cupcakes. Chop the flake bars, if using, into small chunks, then place one chunk of flake or other candy in the center of each cupcake. Keep for 2–3 days in the refrigerator.

Black Forest Cupcakes

Makes 12

1 tbsp unsweetened cocoa
2 tbsp boiling water
1½ cups self-rising flour
1 tsp baking powder
½ cup soft tub margarine
1 cup soft dark brown sugar
2 large eggs
3 tbsp milk

To decorate:

4 oz dark chocolate
4 tbsp seedless raspberry
  jam, warmed
⅔ cup heavy cream
1 tbsp kirsch (optional)
12 natural-colored
  candied cherries

1. Preheat the oven to 350°F. Line a muffin pan with 12 paper baking cups. Blend the unsweetened cocoa with the boiling water and leave to cool.

2. Sift the flour and baking powder into a bowl and add the margarine, sugar, eggs, milk, and the cocoa mixture. Whisk together for about 2 minutes until smooth, then spoon into the baking cups.

3. Bake for 15–20 minutes until springy to the touch. Cool in the pans for 5 minutes, then turn out onto a wire rack to cool.

4. To decorate the cupcakes, melt the chocolate and spread it out to cool on a clean plastic board. When it is almost set, pull a sharp knife through the chocolate to make curls. Refrigerate these until needed. Brush the top of each cupcake with a little raspberry jam. Whisk the cream until it forms soft peaks, then fold in the kirsch, if using. Pipe or swirl the cream on top of each cupcake. Top with chocolate curls and whole candied cherries for the large cupcakes or halved cherries for the small ones. Eat fresh or keep for 1 day in the refrigerator.

Mocha Cupcakes

Makes 12

½ cup soft tub margarine
½ cups superfine sugar (golden,
  if possible)
1¼ cups self-rising flour
2 tbsp unsweetened cocoa
2 large eggs
1 tbsp golden syrup (or corn syrup)
2 tbsp milk

To decorate:
1¾ cups powdered sugar (golden,
  if possible)
½ cup (8 tbsp) unsalted butter, softened
2 tsp coffee extract
12 Cape gooseberries (ground cherries),
  papery covering pulled back

1. Preheat the oven to 350°F. Line a muffin pan with
   12 paper baking cups.

2. Place the margarine and sugar in a large bowl, then sift in
   the flour and unsweetened cocoa.

3. In another bowl, beat the eggs with the syrup, then add
   to the cocoa mixture. Whisk everything together with
   the milk using an electric beater for 2 minutes, or by
   hand with a wooden spoon.

4. Divide the mixture between the baking cups, filling them
   three-quarters full. Bake for about 20 minutes until the
   centers are springy to the touch. Turn out to cool on a
   wire rack.

5. Make the frosting by sifting the powdered sugar into a
   bowl. Add the butter, coffee extract, and 1 tbsp hot water.
   Beat until fluffy, then swirl onto each cupcake with a flat-
   bladed knife. Top each with a fresh Cape gooseberry.
   Keep for up to 2 days in a cool place.

Chocolate & Cranberry Cupcakes

Makes 12

½ cup soft tub margarine
½ cup superfine sugar
  (golden, if possible)
2 large eggs
1½ cups self-rising flour
¼ cup unsweetened cocoa
1 tsp baking powder
2 tbsp milk
¾ cup semisweet chocolate chips
¼ cup dried cranberries

To decorate:
¼ cup unsweetened cocoa
3 tbsp unsalted butter
1 cup golden
  powdered sugar
2 tbsp dried cranberries

1. Preheat the oven to 350°F. Line a muffin pan with
   12 paper baking cups.

2. Place the margarine, sugar, and eggs in a bowl, then sift in
   the flour, unsweetened cocoa, and baking powder. Add
   the milk and beat until smooth, then fold in the chocolate
   chips and cranberries.

3. Spoon into the baking cups and bake for 15–20 minutes
   until firm in the center. Remove to a wire rack to cool.

4. To decorate the cupcakes, blend the unsweetened cocoa
   with 1 tbsp hot water until smooth. Cool for 5 minutes.
   Beat the butter and powdered sugar together and then
   beat in the cocoa mixture.

5. Place in a decorating bag with a plain tip and pipe swirls
   on top of each cupcake. Top with dried cranberries. Keep
   for 2–3 days in the refrigerator.

Rocky Road Cupcakes

Makes 14–18

1 cup self-rising flour
¼ cup unsweetened cocoa
⅔ cup soft dark brown sugar
½ cup soft tub margarine
2 large eggs, beaten
2 tbsp milk

To decorate:
3 oz dark chocolate, broken
 into squares
3 tbsp butter
1⅔ cups mini marshmallows
¼ cup chopped mixed nuts

1. Preheat the oven to 350°F. Line muffin pans with 14–18 paper baking cups or silicone cupcake molds, depending on the depth of the cups or molds.

2. Sift the flour and unsweetened cocoa into a large bowl. Add the sugar, margarine, eggs, and milk and whisk with an electric beater for about 2 minutes until smooth.

3. Divide the mixture evenly between the paper baking cups or the silicone molds and bake for about 20 minutes until a skewer inserted into the middle comes out clean. Remove the pan from the oven but leave the oven on.

4. To make the topping, gently melt the chocolate and butter together in a small saucepan over a low heat. Place the melted chocolate mixture in a decorating bag made of parchment paper and snip off the end. Pipe a little of the mixture on top of each cupcake, then scatter the marshmallows and nuts over each one and return to the oven. Bake for 2–3 minutes to soften the marshmallows. Remove from the oven and pipe the remaining chocolate over the marshmallows. Leave to cool in the pans for 5 minutes, then remove to cool on a wire rack. Serve warm or cold. Keep for up to 2 days in an airtight container.

Chocolate & Orange Marbled Muffins

Makes 10–12

¾ cup soft tub margarine
¾ cup superfine sugar
3 large eggs
1½ cups self-rising flour
1 tsp baking powder
1 tbsp unsweetened cocoa
finely grated zest and juice of ½ orange
4 tbsp runny honey, to glaze

1. Preheat the oven to 350°F. Line muffin pans with 10–12 paper baking cups, or grease 10–12 holes, depending on the depth of the cups.

2. Put the margarine, sugar, eggs, flour, and baking powder into a large mixing bowl. Whisk the mixture together for about 2 minutes until smooth.

3. Place half the mixture into another bowl and sift over the cocoa, then stir in until blended. Stir the orange juice and zest into the other mixture.

4. Spoon the cocoa mixture evenly into the prepared pans or the paper baking cups. Spoon over the orange mixture and, using a flat-bladed knife, swirl through the two mixtures to make a marbled pattern.

5. Bake for 15–20 minutes until well risen and firm to the touch. Cool in the pans for 5 minutes, then turn out to cool on a wire rack. While still warm, drizzle each muffin with a little runny honey. Keep for up to 4 days in an airtight container.

Mint Choc Chip Cupcakes

Makes 12

½ cup soft tub margarine
½ cup superfine sugar (golden,
  if possible)
2 large eggs
1½ cups self-rising flour
¼ cup unsweetened cocoa
1 tsp baking powder
½ cup dark chocolate chips
1 oz clear hard peppermint candies,
  crushed into crumbs

To decorate:
¼ cup (4 tbsp) unsalted butter
1⅓ cups powdered sugar
peppermint flavoring or extract
green food coloring
2 oz dark chocolate squares

1. Preheat the oven to 350°F. Line a muffin pan with
   12 paper baking cups.

2. Place the margarine, sugar, and eggs in a bowl, then sift
   in the flour, unsweetened cocoa, and baking powder. Beat
   by hand or with an electric mixer until smooth, then fold
   in the chocolate chips and the crushed peppermints.

3. Spoon the mixture into the baking cups and bake for
   15–20 minutes until firm in the center. Remove to a wire
   rack to cool.

4. Beat the butter and powdered sugar together with 1 tbsp
   warm water, the peppermint extract, and the food
   coloring. Place in a decorating bag with a star tip and pipe
   swirls on top of each cupcake. Cut the chocolate into
   triangles and place one on top of each cake. Keep for 3–4
   days in an airtight container in a cool place.

Chocolate & Toffee Cupcakes

Makes 12–14

4 oz soft fudge
½ cup soft tub margarine
½ cup superfine sugar (golden, if possible)
1¼ cups self-rising flour
2 tbsp unsweetened cocoa
2 large eggs
1 tbsp golden syrup (or corn syrup)
1 batch cream cheese frosting
  (*see* page 29), to decorate

1. Preheat the oven to 350°F. Line one or two muffin pans with 12–14 paper baking cups, depending on the depth of the cups. Cut one-quarter of the fudge into slices for decoration. Chop the rest into small cubes. Set all the fudge aside.

2. Place the margarine and the sugar in a large bowl and then sift in the flour and unsweetened cocoa. In another bowl, beat the eggs with the syrup, then add to the flour mixture. Whisk together with an electric beater for 2 minutes, or by hand with a wooden spoon, until smooth. Gently fold in the fudge cubes.

3. Spoon the mixture into the baking cups, filling them three-quarters full. Bake for about 15 minutes until a skewer inserted into the center comes out clean. Turn out to cool on a wire rack.

4. Swirl the cream cheese frosting over each cupcake, then finish by topping with a fudge slice. Keep for 3–4 days chilled in an airtight container.

Cappuccino Cupcakes

Makes 12–14

½ cup soft tub margarine
½ cup superfine sugar (golden,
  if possible)
1¼ cups self-rising flour
2 tbsp unsweetened cocoa
2 large eggs
1 tbsp golden syrup (or corn syrup)
scant ½ cup finely dark grated chocolate

To decorate:
⅔ cup heavy cream
½ tsp coffee extract
dark or semisweet
  chocolate sprinkles

1. Preheat the oven to 350°F. Line one or two muffin pans
   with 12–14 paper baking cups or silicone molds,
   depending on the depth of the cups or molds.

2. Place the margarine and the sugar in a large bowl, then
   sift in the flour and unsweetened cocoa.

3. In another bowl, beat the eggs with the syrup, then add to
   the flour mixture. Whisk together with an electric beater
   for 2 minutes, or by hand with a wooden spoon, until
   smooth and then fold in the grated chocolate.

4. Divide the mixture between the baking cups or silicone
   molds, filling them three-quarters full. Bake for about 20
   minutes until springy to the touch in the center. Turn out
   to cool on a wire rack.

5. To decorate, whisk the cream until it forms soft peaks and
   whisk in the coffee extract, then swirl over the tops of the
   muffins with a small metal spatula. Scatter the tops with
   chocolate sprinkles to serve. Eat on the day of decorating
   or keep for 1 day in a sealed container in the refrigerator.

Chunky Chocolate Cupcakes

Makes 12–14

1/2 cup soft tub margarine
1/2 cup superfine sugar
  (golden, if possible)
2 large eggs, beaten
1/4 cup unsweetened cocoa
1 1/2 cups self-rising flour
1 tsp baking powder
2 tbsp milk
1/3 cup semisweet
  chocolate, chopped
1/3 cup dark or white
  chocolate, chopped

To decorate:
heaping 1/2 cup
  granulated sugar
1/3 cup evaporated milk
4 oz dark chocolate,
  chopped
3 tbsp unsalted butter

1. Make the frosting first in order to allow it to cool. Place the sugar and evaporated milk in a heavy-based saucepan and stir over a low heat until every grain of sugar has dissolved. Simmer for 5 minutes but do not allow the mixture to boil. Remove from the heat, cool for 5 minutes, and then add the chocolate and butter. Stir until these melt. Pour the mixture into a bowl and chill for 2 hours until thickened.

2. Preheat the oven to 350°F. Line one or two muffin pans with 12–14 paper baking cups, depending on the depth of the cups. Place the margarine and sugar in a bowl with the eggs and sift in the unsweetened cocoa, flour, and baking powder. Beat with the milk for about 2 minutes until smooth, then fold in the chopped chocolate. Spoon into the baking cups and bake for 15–20 minutes until firm. Place on a wire rack to cool.

3. Remove the frosting from the refrigerator and beat to soften it slightly. Swirl it over the muffins. Keep in a cool place in a sealed container for 3–4 days.

Very Rich Chocolate Cupcakes

Makes 12–14

⅔ cup self-rising flour
¼ cup unsweetened cocoa
⅓ cup soft dark brown sugar
⅓ cup (6 tbsp) butter, softened
3 large eggs
2 tbsp milk

To decorate:
7 oz dark chocolate
½ cup whipping cream
1 tbsp liquid glucose or
  corn syrup
selection chocolate
  decorations

1. Preheat the oven to 350°F. Line one or two muffin pans with 12–14 paper baking cups, depending on the depth of the cups.

2. Sift the flour and unsweetened cocoa into a bowl and add the sugar, butter, eggs, and milk. Whisk until smooth, then spoon into the baking cups.

3. Bake for about 14 minutes until just firm to the touch in the center. Transfer to a wire rack to cool.

4. To decorate the cupcakes, break the chocolate into pieces and melt in a heatproof bowl standing over a saucepan of warm water.

5. In another saucepan, bring the cream to just below boiling, then remove from the heat and stir in the liquid glucose. Add the melted chocolate and stir until smooth and glossy. Spoon over the cupcakes and immediately top each with a chocolate decoration. Leave to set for 30 minutes. Keep for up to 3 days in an airtight container in a cool place.

Orange Drizzle Cupcakes

Makes 10

3 oz dark chocolate, chopped
½ cup (8 tbsp) butter
½ cup superfine sugar
2 large eggs, beaten
1⅔ cups self-rising flour
zest of ½ orange, finely grated
heaping ¼ cup plain Greek yogurt

To decorate:
finely grated zest and
  1 tbsp juice from
  1 small orange
1 batch buttercream
  (*see* page 29)
2 tbsp marmalade

1. Preheat the oven to 375°F. Grease 10 muffin molds or line a muffin pan with 10 paper baking cups.

2. Melt the chocolate in a heatproof bowl over a pan of warm water, or in the microwave oven on low, in bursts of 30 seconds, and leave to cool.

3. Put the butter and sugar in a large bowl and whisk until light and fluffy. Gradually beat in the eggs, adding a teaspoon of flour with each addition. Beat in the cooled melted chocolate, then sift in the remaining flour. Add the orange zest and yogurt to the bowl and whisk until smooth.

4. Spoon the mixture into the prepared pans or the baking cups and bake for about 25 minutes until well risen and springy to the touch. Leave for 2 minutes in the molds or muffin pan, then turn out onto a wire rack.

5. To decorate, mix the orange zest and juice into the buttercream and use to fill a decorating bag fitted with a star tip. Pipe swirls of buttercream on top of each cupcake. Warm the marmalade and place small drizzles over the cupcakes with a teaspoon. Keep in an airtight container in a cool place for up to 4 days.

Parties & Celebration

Boys' & Girls' Names

Makes 16–18

1½ cups self-rising flour
¾ cup superfine sugar
¾ cup soft tub margarine
3 large eggs, beaten
1 tsp vanilla extract

To decorate:
1 batch buttercream
  (*see* page 29)
paste food colorings
sprinkles and decorations
gel piping icing tubes

1. Preheat the oven to 350°F. Line muffin pans with 16–18 spaper baking cups or silicone molds, depending on the depth of the cups or molds.

2. Sift the flour into a bowl and stir together with the superfine sugar. Add the margarine, eggs, and vanilla extract and beat together for about 2 minutes until smooth.

3. Spoon into the baking cups or silicone molds and bake for 15–20 minutes until golden and firm to the touch. Turn out on a wire rack. When cool, trim the tops flat if they have peaked slightly.

4. Divide the buttercream into batches and color pink, green, and yellow. Spread the icing over the cakes. Coat the edges of each cupcake with brightly colored sprinkles or decorations, then add a name in the center of each one with the writing icing. Keep in an airtight container in a cool place for up to 2 days.

Pirate Cupcakes

Makes 14–16

1 cup self-rising flour	To decorate:
½ cup superfine sugar	**4 oz buttercream** (*see* **page 29**)
½ cup soft tub margarine	**1 lb rolled fondant**
2 large eggs, beaten	**pink, yellow, blue, and black**
1 tsp vanilla extract	**paste food coloring**
	powdered sugar, for dusting
	small candies and edible
	colored balls
	small tube red gel piping icing

1. Preheat the oven to 350°F. Line muffin pans with 14–16 paper baking cups or silicone molds, depending on the depth of the cups or molds.

2. Sift the flour into a bowl and stir in the superfine sugar. Add the margarine, eggs, and vanilla extract and beat together for about 2 minutes until smooth. Divide the mixture between the baking cups and bake for 15–20 minutes until golden and firm to the touch. Turn out on a wire rack. When cool, trim the tops flat if they have peaked slightly.

3. To decorate, lightly coat the top of each cupcake with a little buttercream. Color the fondant pale pink and roll out thinly on a surface dusted with powdered sugar. Stamp or cut out circles 2½ inches wide and place these on the buttercream to cover the top of each cupcake.

4. Color some scraps of fondant blue, some yellow, and a small amount black. Make triangular shapes from the blue and yellow fondant and place these onto the pink fondant at an angle to form hats. Stick edible colored balls into the fondant to decorate the hats. Make thin sausages from black fondant and press these across the cupcakes, then make tiny black eye patches. Stick on a tiny candy for each eye and pipe on mouths with the red gel piping icing. Keep for up to 2 days in an airtight container.

Birthday Numbers Cupcakes

Makes 12–14

1 cup self-rising flour
½ cup superfine sugar
½ cup soft tub margarine
2 large eggs, beaten
1 tsp vanilla extract

To decorate:
8 oz rolled fondant
paste food colorings
powdered sugar, for dusting
1 batch buttercream (*see* page 29)
small candles

1. Preheat the oven to 350°F. Line muffin pans with 12–14 paper baking cups or silicone molds, depending on the depth of the cups or molds.

2. Sift the flour into a bowl and stir together with the superfine sugar. Add the margarine, eggs, and vanilla extract and beat together for about 2 minutes until smooth.

3. Spoon into the baking cups or silicone molds and bake for 15–20 minutes until golden and firm to the touch. Turn out on a wire rack. When cool, trim the tops flat if they have peaked slightly.

4. To decorate, color batches of rolled fondant in bright colorings. Dust a clean surface lightly with powdered sugar. Thinly roll each color of fondant and cut out numbers by hand or using a set of cutters. Leave these for 2 hours to dry and harden.

5. Using a metal spatula, spread the buttercream thickly onto the top of each cupcake. Place a small candle into each cupcake and stand the number up against this. Serve within 8 hours because the numbers may start to soften.

Starry Cupcakes

Makes 12

½ cup (8 tbsp)
  butter, softened
½ cup superfine sugar
1 cup self-rising flour
2 large eggs
1 tsp vanilla extract

To decorate:
powdered sugar, for dusting
8 oz rolled fondant
dust or paste food colorings
1 batch cream cheese frosting (*see* page 29)
edible silver ball decorations (optional)
small candles

1. Preheat the oven to 350°F. Line a muffin pan with
   12 paper baking cups.

2. Place the butter and sugar in a bowl, then sift in the flour.
   In another bowl, beat the eggs with the vanilla extract, then
   add to the flour mixture. Beat until smooth, then spoon
   into the baking cups, filling them three-quarters full.

3. Bake for about 18 minutes until firm to the touch in the
   center. Turn out to cool on a wire rack.

4. To decorate the cupcakes, dust a clean flat surface with
   powdered sugar. Color the fondant in batches of bright
   colors, such as blue, yellow, and orange. Roll each out
   thinly and cut out stars by hand or with a cutter. Leave
   to dry out for 2 hours until firm. Place the frosting in a
   decorating bag fitted with a star tip and pipe large swirls
   on top of each cupcake. Decorate each cupcake with
   stars, edible silver balls, if using, and small candles. Keep
   for up to 2 days in an airtight container in a cool place.

New Home Cupcakes

Makes 14

1 cup self-rising flour	**To decorate:**
½ cup superfine sugar	4 oz buttercream (*see* page 29)
½ cup soft tub margarine	powdered sugar, for dusting
2 large eggs, beaten	1 lb rolled fondant
1 tsp vanilla extract	red, brown, and yellow paste
	food colorings
	white gel piping icing tubes

1. Preheat the oven to 350°F. Line muffin pans with 14 paper baking cups or silicone molds.

2. Sift the flour into a bowl and stir together with the superfine sugar. Add the margarine, eggs, and vanilla extract and beat together for about 2 minutes until smooth.

3. Spoon into the baking cups or silicone molds and bake for 15–20 minutes until golden and firm to the touch. Turn out on a wire rack. When cool, trim the tops flat if they have peaked slightly and lightly coat the top of each cupcake with a little buttercream.

4. To decorate, dust a clean flat surface with powdered sugar. Color half the rolled fondant a pale lemon yellow and roll it out thinly. Cut out circles 2½ inches wide and place these over the buttercream and press to smooth down. Color half the remaining fondant brown and the other half red. Roll out thinly on a dusted surface. Cut out small squares in the brown icing and triangular roof shapes in red icing. Press the shapes onto the cupcakes and pipe on doors, windows, and roof tiles in white piping icing. Keep for up to 3 days in an airtight container.

Polka Dot Cupcakes

Makes 12

²⁄₃ cup (1¼ sticks)
  butter, softened
²⁄₃ cup superfine sugar
1½ cups self-rising flour
3 large eggs
1 tsp vanilla extract
2 tbsp milk

To decorate:
1 batch cream cheese
  frosting (*see* page 29)
4 oz rolled fondant
paste food colorings

1. Preheat the oven to 350°F. Line a muffin pan with 12 paper baking cups.

2. Place the butter and sugar in a bowl, then sift in the flour. In another bowl, beat the eggs with the vanilla extract and milk, then add to the flour mixture and beat until smooth. Spoon into the baking cups, filling them three-quarters full.

3. Bake for about 18 minutes until firm to the touch in the center. Turn out to cool on a wire rack.

4. To decorate the cupcakes, swirl the top of each cupcake with a little cream cheese frosting using a small metal spatula. Divide the fondant into batches and color each one separately with paste food coloring. Dust a clean flat surface with powdered sugar. Roll out the colored fondant and stamp out small colored circles with the flat end of a decorating bag tip. Press the dots onto the frosting. Keep for up to 3 days in a cool place in an airtight container.

Valentine Heart Cupcakes

Makes 12

⅔ cup (1¼ sticks)
  butter, softened
⅔ cup superfine sugar
3 large eggs, beaten
1 tsp vanilla extract
2 tbsp milk
1¼ cups self-rising flour
½ tsp baking powder

To decorate:
pink and red paste
  food coloring
8 oz rolled fondant
powdered sugar, for dusting
1 batch cream cheese frosting
  (*see* page 29)

1. Preheat the oven to 350°F and line a muffin pan with 12 paper baking cups.

2. Place the butter, sugar, eggs, vanilla extract, and milk in a bowl, then sift in the flour and baking powder. Beat together for about 2 minutes with an electric hand mixer until pale and fluffy. Spoon into the baking cups and bake for 20–25 minutes until firm and golden. Cool on a wire rack.

3. To decorate, color one third of the fondant pink and one third red, leaving the rest white. Dust a clean flat surface with powdered sugar. Roll out the fondant thinly and cut out pink, red, and white heart shapes, then leave to dry flat and harden for 2 hours.

4. Color the cream cheese frosting pale pink and place in a decorating bag fitted with a star tip. Pipe a swirl on top of each cupcake and decorate with the hearts. Keep in a cool place for up to 2 days.

Mother's Day Rose Cupcakes

Makes 12

½ cup superfine sugar
½ cup soft tub margarine
2 large eggs
1 cup self-rising flour
1 tsp baking powder
1 tsp rosewater

To decorate:
2 oz rolled fondant
pink paste food coloring
2¾ cups fondant sugar or
  powdered sugar

1. Preheat the oven to 375°F. Line a muffin pan with 12 paper baking cups.

2. Place all the cupcake ingredients in a large bowl and beat with an electric mixer for about 2 minutes until smooth. Fill the baking cups halfway up with the batter. Bake for about 15 minutes until firm, risen, and golden. Remove to a wire rack to cool.

3. To decorate the cupcakes, first line an egg carton with foil and set aside. Color the fondant with pink paste food coloring. Make a small cone shape, then roll a pea-sized piece of fondant into a ball. Flatten out the ball into a petal shape and wrap this around the cone shape. Continue adding more petals to make a rose, then trim the thick base, place in the egg carton and leave to dry out for 2 hours.

4. Blend the fondant sugar or powdered sugar with a little water to make a thick icing of spreading consistency, then color this pale pink. Smooth over the top of each cupcake and decorate with the roses immediately. Leave to set for 1 hour. Keep for 1 day in an airtight container.

Father's Day Cupcakes

Makes 14

1 cup self-rising flour
½ cup superfine sugar
½ cup soft tub margarine
2 large eggs, beaten
1 tsp vanilla extract

To decorate:
1 batch buttercream (*see* page 29)
blue, yellow, and orange paste
   food colorings
powdered sugar, for dusting
8 oz rolled fondant
½ cup royal icing mix
edible silver balls

1. Preheat the oven to 350°F. Line muffin pans with 14 paper baking cups or silicone molds.

2. Sift the flour into a bowl and stir in the superfine sugar. Add the margarine, eggs, and vanilla extract and beat together for about 2 minutes until smooth.

3. Spoon into the baking cups or silicone molds and bake for 15–20 minutes until golden and firm to the touch. Turn out on a wire rack. When cool, trim the tops flat if they have peaked slightly.

4. To decorate, color half the buttercream yellow and the other half orange and swirl over the top of each cupcake. Dust a clean flat surface with powdered sugar. Color the fondant light blue and roll out thinly. Stamp or cut out large stars 1½ inches wide and place these on the buttercream.

5. Make the royal icing mix and place in a paper decorating bag with the end snipped off and pipe "Dad" or names on the stars. Decorate with the edible silver balls. Keep for up to 3 days in an airtight container.

Butterfly Wings & Flowers Cupcakes

Makes 12–14

²⁄₃ cup (1¼ sticks)
  butter, softened
²⁄₃ cup superfine sugar
1½ cups self-rising flour
3 large eggs, beaten
1 tsp lemon juice
2 tbsp milk

To decorate:
12 oz rolled fondant
paste food colorings
powdered sugar, for dusting
1 batch cream cheese
  frosting (*see* page 29)
gel piping icing tubes

1. Preheat the oven to 350°F. Line one or two muffin pans with 12–14 paper baking cups, depending on the depth of the cups.

2. Place the butter and sugar in a bowl, then sift in the flour. Add the beaten eggs to the bowl with the lemon juice and milk and beat until smooth. Spoon into the baking cups, filling them three-quarters full.

3. Bake for about 18 minutes until firm to the touch in the center. Turn out to cool on a wire rack.

4. To decorate, color the fondant in batches of lilac, blue, pink, and yellow. Dust a clean flat surface with powdered sugar. Roll out the fondant thinly and mark out butterfly wings, and daisy shapes with a fluted daisy cutter. Leave these to dry for 30 minutes until firm enough to handle.

5. Place the frosting in a decorating bag fitted with a star tip and pipe swirls onto each cupcake. Press the wings and flowers onto the frosting and pipe on decorations with small gel piping icing tubes. Keep in an airtight container in a cool place for up to 3 days.

Silver Wedding Celebration Cupcakes

Makes 24

⅔ cup (1¼ sticks)
  butter, softened
⅔ cup superfine sugar
1¼ cups self-rising flour
¼ cup ground almonds
3 large eggs, beaten
1 tsp almond extract
2 tbsp milk

To decorate:
12 oz rolled fondant
edible silver dusting powder
1 lb fondant sugar or
  powdered sugar
24 small silver ribbon bows

1. Preheat the oven to 350°F. Line two muffin pans with 24 silver foil baking cups.

2. Place the butter and sugar in a bowl, then sift in the flour and stir in the almonds. Add the beaten eggs to the bowl along with the almond extract and milk and beat until smooth. Spoon into the baking cups, filling them three-quarters full.

3. Bake for about 18 minutes until firm to the touch in the center. Turn out onto a wire rack. Once cool, trim the tops of the cupcakes if they have peaked.

4. To decorate the cupcakes, first line an egg carton with foil. Roll the fondant into pea-sized balls and mold each one into a petal shape. Mold a cone shape and wrap a petal completely around this. Take another petal and wrap around the first, overlapping. Continue wrapping 4–5 petals around until a rose has formed. Pull the thick base away, flute out the petals and place in the egg carton. Repeat until you have 24 roses. Leave them to dry out for 2–4 hours. When they are firm, brush edible silver dusting powder lightly over each rose with a clean paintbrush.

5. Mix the fondant sugar or powdered sugar with water, according to the package instructions, to a thick spreading consistency. Spread over the top of each cupcake. This icing will set, so work quickly. Press a rose into the icing and place a thin silver bow on each cupcake. Leave to set for 30 minutes. Keep in a cool place for up to 2 days. Remove the bows before eating.

Golden Wedding Celebration Cupcakes

Makes 24

1 cup self-rising flour	**To decorate:**
½ cup superfine sugar	**4 oz buttercream** (*see* **page 29**)
½ cup soft tub margarine	**powdered sugar, for dusting**
2 large eggs, beaten	**1½ lb rolled fondant**
1 tsp lemon juice	**yellow paste food coloring**
	thin gold ribbon, curled

1. Preheat the oven to 350°F. Line two muffin pans with 24 gold foil baking cups.

2. Sift the flour into a bowl and stir together with the superfine sugar. Add the margarine and eggs and beat together with the lemon juice for about 2 minutes until smooth.

3. Spoon into the baking cups and bake for 15–20 minutes until golden and firm to the touch. Turn out on a wire rack. When cool, trim the tops flat if they have peaked slightly.

4. To decorate, lightly coat the top of each cupcake with a little buttercream. Dust a clean flat surface with powdered sugar. Roll out two thirds of the fondant and stamp or cut out circles 2½ inches wide and place these on the buttercream to cover the top of each cupcake.

5. Color one eighth of the fondant a deep yellow and mold this into thin sausage shapes. Leave these to dry for about 2 hours until firm. Roll out the remaining white fondant and mark out small squares ¾ x ¾ inch. Wrap a square around a yellow center to form a lily and press the ends together. Make all the lilies and place on the cupcakes. Cut short thin strips of gold paper ribbon and pull along the blade of a pair of scissors to curl and place on the cakes. Keep for up to 3 days in an airtight container in a cool place. Remove the ribbons before eating.

Bluebird Cupcakes

Makes 12–14

⅔ cup (1¼ sticks)
  butter, softened
⅔ cup superfine sugar
1¼ cups self-rising flour
3 large eggs, beaten
1 tsp lemon juice
1 tbsp milk

To decorate:
4 oz rolled fondant
blue paste food coloring
powdered sugar, for dusting
1 batch cream cheese frosting
  (*see* page 29)
white gel piping icing tube

1. Preheat the oven to 350°F. Line one or two muffin pans with 12–14 paper baking cups, depending on the depth of the cups.

2. Place the butter and sugar in a bowl, then sift in the flour. Add the eggs to the bowl with the lemon juice and milk and beat until smooth. Spoon into the baking cups, filling them three-quarters full.

3. Bake for about 18 minutes until firm to the touch in the center. Turn out to cool on a wire rack.

4. To decorate the cupcakes, color the fondant blue. Dust a clean flat surface with powdered sugar. Roll out the fondant thinly and mark out bird wings in sets of two and one body per bird, then stamp out some daisy shapes. Leave all these to dry out for 30 minutes until firm enough to handle.

5. Swirl the frosting onto each cupcake. Press one bird's body and pair of wings, and some flowers, onto the frosting and pipe on decorations with the white gel icing. Keep in an airtight container in a cool place for up to 3 days.

Easter Nest Cupcakes

Makes 12

½ cup soft tub margarine
½ cup superfine sugar (golden,
  if possible)
1¼ cups self-rising flour
2 tbsp unsweetened cocoa
2 large eggs
1 tbsp golden syrup (or corn syrup)

To decorate:
1 batch buttercream (*see* page 29)
2 "biscuits" (or 1 cup spoon-sized)
  shredded wheat cereal
4 oz semisweet chocolate,
  broken into pieces
2 tbsp unsalted butter
chocolate mini eggs

1. Preheat the oven to 350°F. Line a muffin pan with
   12 paper baking cups.

2. Place the margarine and the sugar in a large bowl, then
   sift in the flour and unsweetened cocoa. In another bowl,
   beat the eggs with the syrup, then add to the first bowl.
   Whisk together with an electric beater for 2 minutes, or
   by hand with a wooden spoon, until smooth.

3. Spoon the mixture into the baking cups, filling them
   three-quarters full. Bake for about 15 minutes until they
   are springy to the touch in the center. Turn out to cool
   on a wire rack.

4. To decorate, swirl the buttercream over the top of each
   cupcake. Break up the shredded wheat finely. Melt the
   chocolate with the butter, then stir in the shredded wheat
   and let cool slightly. Line a plate with plastic wrap. Mold
   the mixture into tiny nest shapes with your fingers, then
   place them on the lined plate. Freeze for a few minutes
   to harden. Set a nest on top of each cupcake and fill
   with mini eggs. Keep for up to 2 days in a cool place in
   an airtight container.

Harvest Festival Cupcakes

Makes 12

1½ cups self-rising
  whole-wheat flour
1 tsp baking powder
½ tsp ground cinnamon
pinch salt
⅔ cup corn oil or canola oil
⅔ cup soft light brown sugar
3 large eggs, beaten
1 tsp vanilla extract
½ cup golden raisins
3 carrots, 8–9 inches long,
  peeled and finely grated

To decorate:
1 batch cream cheese
  frosting (*see* page 29)
paste food colorings
8 oz rolled fondant

1. Preheat the oven to 350°F. Lightly oil a muffin pan or line with 12 paper baking cups.

2. Sift the flour, baking powder cinnamon, and salt into a bowl, along with any wheat germ from the sieve.

3. Add the oil, sugar, eggs, vanilla extract, golden raisins, and grated carrots. Beat until smooth and then spoon into the prepared pan or baking cups. Bake for 20–25 minutes until risen and golden. Cool on a wire rack.

4. To decorate, color the frosting pale green and smooth over the top of each cupcake. Color the fondant in small batches of orange, red, green, and brown and mold into cabbages, carrots, potatoes, and tomatoes. Press green fondant through a garlic crusher to make green carrot leaves. Place the vegetables on top of each cupcake. Keep for up to 3 days in an airtight container in a cool place.

Halloween Cobweb Cupcakes

Makes 16–18

¾ cup superfine sugar
¾ cup soft tub margarine
3 large eggs, beaten
1¼ cups self-rising flour
1 tsp baking powder
¼ cup unsweetened cocoa

To decorate:
1¾ cups powdered
   sugar, sifted
2 tbsp warm water
orange and black paste
   food colorings

1. Preheat the oven to 350°F. Line muffin pans with
   16–18 paper or foil baking cups, depending on the
   depth of the cups.

2. Place the sugar, margarine, and eggs in a bowl, then sift
   in the flour, baking powder, and unsweetened cocoa.
   Beat for 2 minutes, or until smooth.

3. Spoon the mixture into the baking cups and bake for
   15–20 minutes until well risen and the tops spring back
   when lightly pressed. Transfer to a wire rack to cool, then
   trim the tops of the cupcakes flat if they have any peaks.

4. To decorate the cupcakes, gradually mix the powdered sugar
   with enough warm water to give a coating consistency.
   Color a little of the icing black and place in a small paper
   decorating bag. Color the remaining icing bright orange.

5. Work on one cupcake at a time. Spread orange icing
   over the top of the cupcake. Snip a small hole from the
   base of the decorating bag, then pipe a black spiral on top
   of the wet orange icing. Use a wooden toothpick and pull
   this through the icing to give a cobweb effect. Repeat
   with all the cupcakes and leave to set for 1 hour. Keep for
   up to 2 days in an airtight container in a cool place.

Sparkly Snowflake Cupcakes

Makes 24

²/₃ cup (1¼ sticks) butter, softened
1 cup superfine sugar
1¼ cups self-rising flour
¼ cup ground almonds
3 large eggs, beaten
1 tsp almond extract
1 tbsp milk

To decorate:
powdered sugar, for dusting
12 oz rolled fondant
4½ cups royal icing mix
edible silver balls

1. Preheat the oven to 350°F. Line two muffin pans with 24 silver foil baking cups.

2. Place the butter and sugar in a bowl, then sift in the flour and stir in the almonds. Add the beaten eggs to the bowl with the almond extract and milk. Spoon into the baking cups, filling them three-quarters full.

3. Bake for about 18 minutes until firm to the touch in the center. Turn out onto a wire rack. Once cool, trim the tops of the cupcakes if they have peaked.

4. To decorate the cupcakes, dust a clean flat surface with powdered sugar. Roll out the fondant thinly and mark out snowflake patterns. Cut around the shapes and leave them to dry flat on a sheet of nonstick parchment paper for 2 hours until firm.

5. Make the royal icing mix according to the package instructions to a soft icing that will form peaks. Swirl the icing onto the cupcakes and place a snowflake shape centrally on each one. Decorate with silver balls and leave for 30 minutes to set. Keep for up to 2 days in an airtight container.

Festive Candy Cane Cupcakes

Makes 14–18

²⁄₃ cup (1¼ sticks)
  butter, softened
²⁄₃ cup superfine sugar
1¼ cups self-rising flour
¼ cup ground almonds
3 large eggs, beaten
1 tsp vanilla extract
2 tbsp milk

To decorate:
8 oz rolled fondant
red and green paste
  food colorings
powdered sugar, for dusting
1 lb royal icing mix

1. Preheat the oven to 350°F. Line muffin pans with 14–18 foil baking cups, depending on the depth of the cups.

2. Place the butter and sugar in a bowl, then sift in the flour and stir in the almonds. Add the eggs to the bowl along with the vanilla extract and milk. Spoon into the baking cups, filling them three-quarters full. Bake for about 18 minutes until firm to the touch in the center. Turn out onto a wire rack. Once cool, trim the tops of the cupcakes if they have peaked.

3. To decorate, color one quarter of the fondant red and one quarter green. Dust a clean flat surface with powdered sugar. Roll out the fondant into long, very thin sausages with the palms of your hands. Twist a sausage of red with a sausage of white, cut into short lengths about 2½ inches long, and bend round to form a cane shape. Repeat with green and white fondant. Leave to dry out flat for 2 hours until firm.

4. Make the royal icing according to the package instructions to a soft icing that will form peaks. Smooth the icing onto the cupcakes and place a cane centrally on each one. Place the remaining icing in a small decorating bag fitted with a star tip and pipe a star border around the outside of each cupcake. Keep for up to 2 days in an airtight container.

Hanukkah Honey Spice Cupcakes

Makes 12–14

1 tsp instant coffee granules
⅓ cup hot water
1½ cups all-purpose flour
1 tsp baking powder
½ tsp baking soda
½ tsp ground cinnamon
½ tsp ground ginger
pinch ground cloves
2 large eggs
½ cup superfine sugar (golden, if possible)
½ cup honey
⅓ cup vegetable oil
⅓ cup walnuts, finely chopped
1¼ cups powdered sugar (golden, if possible), to decorate

1. Preheat the oven to 325°F. Line one or two muffin pans with
   12–14 paper baking cups, depending on the depth of the cups.
   Dissolve the coffee in the water and leave aside to cool.

2. Sift the flour with the baking powder, baking soda, and spices.
   In another bowl, beat the eggs with the sugar and honey until
   smooth and light, then gradually beat in the oil until blended.
   Stir this into the flour mixture along with the coffee and
   walnuts. Beat until smooth.

3. Carefully spoon the mixture into the baking cups. Fill each
   halfway up. Be careful not to overfill them because the batter
   will rise up. Bake for 25–30 minutes until they are risen, firm,
   and golden. Leave in the pans for 5 minutes, then turn out
   onto a wire rack to cool.

4. To decorate, blend the powdered sugar with 1 tbsp warm
   water to make a thin glacé icing. Place in a paper decorating
   bag and snip off the tip. Pipe Hanukkah symbols or flowers
   over each cupcake and leave to set for 30 minutes. Keep in
   an airtight container for up to 5 days.

Giftwrapped Presents Cupcakes

Makes 12–14

½ cup (8 tbsp) butter
1¼ cups soft dark muscovado sugar
2 large eggs, beaten
1 cup self-rising flour
1 tsp ground pumpkin pie spice
finely grated zest and 1 tbsp juice from 1 orange
1 tbsp molasses
2¼ cups mixed dried fruit

To decorate:
3 tbsp sieved apricot glaze (*see* page 31)
powdered sugar, for dusting
1 lb 5 oz rolled fondant
red, blue, green, and yellow paste
  food colorings

1. Preheat the oven to 350°F. Line one or two muffin pans with
   12–14 paper baking cups, depending on the depth of the cups.

2. Beat the butter and sugar together until light and fluffy, then
   beat in the eggs a little at a time, adding 1 tsp flour with each
   addition. Sift in the remaining flour and spice, add the orange
   zest and juice, molasses, and dried fruit to the bowl and fold
   together until the mixture is blended.

3. Spoon into the baking cups and bake for about 30 minutes until
   firm in the center and a skewer comes out clean. Leave to cool
   in the pans for 15 minutes, then turn out to cool on a wire
   rack. Store undecorated in an airtight container for up to 4
   weeks, or freeze until needed.

4. To decorate, trim the top of each cupcake level if they have
   peaked, then brush with apricot glaze. Dust a clean flat surface
   with powdered sugar. Color the fondant in batches and roll out
   thinly. Cut out circles 2½ inches wide. Place a disk on top of
   each cupcake and press level. Mold colored scraps into long thin
   sausages and roll these out thinly. Place a contrasting color across
   each cupcake and arrange into bows and loops. Leave to dry for
   24 hours if possible. Keep for up to 4 days in an airtight container.

Crystallized Rosemary & Cranberry Cupcakes

Makes 12

1 cup self-rising flour
½ cup (8 tbsp)
   butter, softened
½ cup golden
   superfine sugar
2 large eggs, beaten
zest of ½ orange,
   finely grated

To decorate:
1 egg white
12 small rosemary sprigs
1¼ cups fresh cranberries
superfine sugar, for dusting
3 tbsp apricot glaze, sieved
   (*see* page 31)
12 oz rolled fondant
powdered sugar, for dusting

1. Preheat the oven to 350°F. Line a muffin pan with 12 foil baking cups.

2. Sift the flour into a bowl and add the butter, sugar, eggs, and orange zest. Beat for about 2 minutes until smooth, then spoon into the baking cups.

3. Bake in the center of the oven for about 14 minutes until well risen and springy in the center. Transfer to a wire rack to cool.

4. To decorate, place a sheet of nonstick parchment paper on a flat surface. Beat the egg white until frothy, then brush thinly over the rosemary and cranberries and place them on the nonstick parchment paper. Dust with superfine sugar and leave to dry out for 2–4 hours until crisp.

5. Brush the top of each cupcake with a little apricot glaze. Roll out the fondant on a clean flat surface dusted with powdered sugar and cut out 12 circles 2½ inches wide. Place a disk on top of each cupcake, and press level. Decorate each one with sparkly rosemary sprigs and cranberries. Keep for up to 3 days in an airtight container in a cool place.

White Chocolate Christmas Cupcakes

Makes 12–16

²/₃ cup (1¼ sticks) butter, softened
²/₃ cup superfine sugar
1¼ cups self-rising flour
3 large eggs, beaten
1 tsp vanilla extract
1 tbsp milk
scant ²/₃ cup finely grated
  white chocolate

To decorate:
²/₃ cup chopped white chocolate
16 holly leaves, cleaned and dried
1 batch buttercream (*see* page 29)
powdered sugar, for dusting

1. Preheat the oven to 350°F. Line one or two muffin pans with 12–16 foil baking cups, depending on the depth of the cups.

2. Place the butter and sugar in a bowl, then sift in the flour. Add the eggs to the bowl with the vanilla extract and milk and beat until smooth. Fold in the grated white chocolate, then spoon into the baking cups, filling them three-quarters full.

3. Bake for about 18 minutes until firm to the touch in the center. Turn out to cool on a wire rack.

4. To decorate, melt the white chocolate in a heatproof bowl standing over a pan of barely simmering water. Use one third of the melted chocolate to paint the underside of the holly leaves and leave to set for 30 minutes in the refrigerator. Spread one third of the chocolate out onto a clean plastic board. When almost set, make into curls by pulling a sharp knife through the chocolate at an angle until the chocolate curls away from the knife. Stir the remaining cooled chocolate into the buttercream and chill for 15 minutes.

5. Swirl each cupcake with buttercream, then press on the white chocolate curls. Peel the holly leaves away from the chocolate and carefully place on top of the cupcakes. Dust with powdered sugar before serving. Keep for up to 2 days in the refrigerator.